Anxious Learning

Effects of Anxiety on Cognitive Functions

Thomas Hodge

To those who ask questions,
To those who break the mold,
To those who challenge the system.

Table of Contents

Abstract

Anxiety is known to affect the cognitive process of the mind. Explanations on the effects of anxiety on these processes have been refined through increasingly more detailed cognitive theories. The theories began as generalized views of anxiety being a distractor as could be seen in the concept of cognitive bias (Calvo and Eysenck, 1998). Research has provided an explanation that anxiety affected the functions of the central executive in the processing efficacy theory. Attentional control theory refined processing efficacy theory's explanation of anxiety. Attentional control theory pinpointed specific functions affected by anxiety. The theory shows that anxiety which is not related to the individual's present goal can impair shifting and inhibition functions in cognitive processing, but research into attentional control theory has shown that is related to the current goal anxiety causes an increase in processing efficacy (Causer, Holmes, Smith, and Williams, 2011). Understanding the different impacts of anxiety and how it relates to the individual and the goal at hand can serve to improve efficiency in functioning, learning, and responses of an individual. Further research concerning the refinement of current theories is discussed.

Effects of Anxiety on Cognitive Functions

Anxiety is a state that is characterized by emotional, behavioral, cognitive, and physical effects on an individual. Derakshan and Eysenck (2009) described anxiety as, "an aversive motivational state that occurs in situations in which level of perceived threat to the individual is high" (p. 168). Since anxiety is based on a perceived threat to an individual, anxiety could have an impact on thought processes due to it being an imagined threat created by higher-level thought processes that exists as a part of one's perception and understanding of reality. Research on the effects of anxiety would be potentially beneficial by providing an understanding about how the presence of anxiety affects learning and the degree to which anxiety can be present for optimal performance of an individual in processing information.

The ability of an individual to learn information is dependent upon the individual's attention to learning the new information, ability to store the information, and the recalling of the information. In cognitive theory, working memory is a crucial element in these processes. "Working memory refers to the temporary storage of information that is necessary for performing cognitive tasks such as comprehension, reasoning and learning" (Grimley, Dahraei, and Riding, 2008, p. 213). In other words, the working memory is the cognitive system that holds information over a period of seconds for the purpose of completing tasks that are normally goal-oriented in some way. For example, working memory is crucial in the task of learning as it allows one to hold one smaller concept in thought to be combined with other small concepts so that an individual can learn a more complex concept.

A primary cognitive structure that relates to the processes of working memory is the central executive. Smith and Jonides (as cited in Derakshan and Eysenck, 2009) explained that the central executive functioned in the directing, changing, and inhibiting of attention in relation to tasks by refreshing of contents in the working memory and reorganizing the representations that exist in working memory. In other words, the central executive function is essentially the coordinating feature of the working memory that chooses the information to be learned, switches the focus of learning between items, and selects what information will not be learned. The executive function coordinates the phonological loop for audible information and the visuospatial sketchpad for visual information.

Cognitive Bias

The concept of cognitive bias is important in understanding the concept of how anxiety affects working memory. Calvo and Eysenck (1998) explained that cognitive bias was a reaction to threat-related stimuli. The cognitive functioning which is directed by the central executive would direct more focus toward the stimuli that are perceived as a threat as opposed to stimuli that are not perceived to be a threat. This redirection of attention would have the possibility of reducing an individual's ability to learn information if the information to be learned is perceived as being lesser of a threat than other information. The concept illustrates a bias of the central function toward certain thought processes based on the threat level associated with different stimuli.

Processing Efficacy Theory

Processing efficacy theory built on the concept of cognitive bias by attempting to explain a relationship between anxiety and the efficiency of processing in individuals. Derakshan and Eysenck (2009) explained that processing efficacy theory assumed, "Anxiety typically impairs processing efficiency to a greater extent than performance effectiveness" (p. 169). The theory made connections between anxiety levels and processing information. The processing efficacy theory attempted to correlate the relationship between anxiety levels and the performances tasks associated with the specific systems that respond to the central executive, such as the phonological loop or the visuospatial sketchpad.

Processing efficacy theory explains that higher anxiety levels impair cognitive processing efficacy, but the theory does not provide details concerning how the functions of the central executive, such as directing, changing, and inhibiting attention, that are affected by anxiety.

Attentional Control Theory

The attentional control theory builds on the processing efficacy theory by addressing the specific functions of the central executive. Eysenck, Derakshan, Santos, and Calvo (2007) explain that "Anxiety impairs attentional control, a key function of the central executive. It follows that anxious individuals preferentially allocate attentional resources to threat-related stimuli whether internal (e.g., worrisome thoughts) or external (e.g., threatening task-irrelevant distractors)" (p. 338). The attentional control theory uses the concept of cognitive bias to attempt to provide a basis of understanding as to how anxiety has an impact on the cognitive functions of an individual. The theory is similar to the processing efficacy theory as it attempts to explain the relationship between anxiety and cognitive processing.

Attentional control theory provides an explanation of which specific functions of the central executive anxiety affects which was on one of the shortcomings of the processing efficacy theory. Eysenck et al. (2007) identify the shifting and inhibition functions as the primary central executive functions affected by anxiety. The effect on the functions can be seen in the way subjects were more easily distracted in an anxious state as opposed to subjects in nonanxious states. This inability to focus one's attention while in anxious state can be seen as a sign of a decreased ability to block out unrelated stimuli due to an impaired inhibition function.

Anxiety can have positive effects on the abilities of an individual to accomplish tasks under certain circumstances concerning the type of anxiety. Causer, Holmes, Smith, and Williams (2011) explained, "Those individuals who are in an anxious state frequently worry about the threat to a current goal and attempt to develop strategies to reduce the effects of anxiety and ultimately complete the goal" (p. 595). In the study conducted by Causer et al. (2011), the optical focus of competitive marksmen under states of low and high anxiety was measured to determine differences in reaction time by the participants. The anxiety that was simulated for the individuals had a direct connection to the task to be completed. Due to the anxiety being directly related to the task, the individuals would focus more specifically on the task due to the anxiety's relationship to the task. The presence of the anxiety resulted in the central function of the individuals directing more of their focus toward accomplishing the task due to the presence of a perceived threat toward their goal at the time. The presence of anxiety assisted the individuals in blocking out irrelevant stimuli by inhibiting attentional shifts away from the goal due to the fact that the anxiety and goal of individual combined to attract more of the individual's attention than the goal would by itself.

Many other researchers utilized techniques of measuring eye movements and behavioral processes to determine the effects of anxiety on working memory. Derakshan and Eysenck (2009) compiled several studies to find that anxiety impaired the shifting and inhibiting functions of the central executive along with processing efficiency. The impairment of central executive functions can cause cognitive confusion which would increase the level of anxiety in the individual as shown in the studies of Grimley et al. (2008). This perpetuation of anxiety could cause problems with cognitive functioning in individuals as the anxiety would direct an excess degree of focus toward threat related stimuli causing a difficulty in shifting attention between stimuli.

Discussion

Research into the effects of anxiety on cognitive performance has yielded evidence that the context of the anxiety affects how efficacy is impacted by anxiety. Eysenck (as cited in Calvo and Eysenck, 1998) explained that the discrepancies found could be attributed to bias-related functions that relate to the attentional process and the interpretation of information due to internal sources. In the research by Causer et al. (2011), results were found showing high-anxiety individuals had quicker reactionary times than low-anxiety individuals. This was attributed to how the high-anxiety individuals utilized internal cues to give cognitive preference to the goals that were perceived to be threatened by anxiety. In this particular experiment, the anxiety was perceived as a threat toward the goal. This provides a look at how anxiety serves to improve the functioning of an individual in the case of anxiety causing an individual to focus cognitive efforts toward a goal instead of causing the individual to experience difficulties in maintain a focus toward the goal. In consideration of the differing effects of anxiety, one could manipulate the levels and perception of anxiety to improve focus and functioning as opposed to viewing anxiety as an impairment to functioning.

Further research into the effects of anxiety on cognitive function can be highly beneficial by provide educators with a better understanding of how various types of anxiety can direct learning and cognitive processing as related to a specific goal. The research shows that different types of anxiety produce different results. Differing quantities of anxiety should produce different results when examining the idea logically. To fully the cognitive theories concerning the effects of anxiety, research concerning how different levels of anxiety that affect efficacy would serve to provide a better understanding of whether different levels of anxiety improve or impair efficacy.

Summary

In summary, the cognitive theories of how anxiety affects the functioning of an individual can be seen as growing and expanding theories. The concept of cognitive bias provided an understanding as to how the central executive would direct its focus toward threats as opposed to neutral stimuli (Calvo and Eysenck, 1998). The processing efficacy theory built on the concept of cognitive bias to provide an understanding that anxiety impaired the ability of the individual to process thoughts and inputs by decreasing the effective rate for which an individual performs cognitive tasks (Derakshan and Eysenck, 2009). Processing efficacy theory laid the ground work for the attentional control theory. The attentional control theory combined these two concepts to formulate the way in which anxiety specifically affected cognitive functions. The shifting and inhibition functions of the central executive were the two specific functions that were affected (Eysenck et al., 2007). Attentional control theorists concluded that the impairment of certain functions could be directed in such a way to improve task efficacy of an individual (Causer et al., 2011). The determination as to whether the anxiety serves to impair or improve performance depends on whether the anxiety detracts attention from the goal or directs attention toward the goal. Implications of further research into attentional control theory could benefit educators and industry in allowing a better understanding of what type of anxiety to allow during learning and what quantity of anxiety should be present.

References

Calvo, M. G., & Eysenck, M. W. (1998). Cognitive Bias to Internal Sources of Information in Anxiety. *International Journal of Psychology, 33*(4), 287-299. doi:10.1080/002075998400321

Causer, J., Holmes, P. S., Smith, N. C., & Williams, A. (2011). Anxiety, movement kinematics, and visual attention in elite-level performers. *Emotion, 11*(3), 595-602. doi:10.1037/a0023225

Derakshan, N., & Eysenck, M. W. (2009). Anxiety, processing efficiency, and cognitive performance: New developments from attentional control theory. *European Psychologist, 14*(2), 168-176. doi:10.1027/1016-9040.14.2.168

Eysenck, M. W., Derakshan, N., Santos, R., & Calvo, M. G. (2007). Anxiety and cognitive performance: Attentional control theory.

Emotion, 7(2), 336-353. doi:10.1037/1528-3542.7.2.336

Grimley, M., Dahraei, H., & Riding, R. J. (2008). The relationship between anxiety-stability, working memory and cognitive style. *Educational Studies*, *34*(3), 213-223. doi:10.1080/03055690701811339